WIPO IP Facts and Figures 2022

WIPO
WORLD
INTELLECTUAL PROPERTY
ORGANIZATION

Suggested citation: WIPO (2022). *IP Facts and Figures 2022*. Geneva: World Intellectual Property Organization. DOI: 10.34667/tind.47183

First published 2022

World Intellectual Property Organization
34, chemin des Colombettes
P.O. Box 18
CH-1211 Geneva 20
Switzerland

ISBN: 978-92-805-3500-6 (print)
ISBN: 978-92-805-3501-3 (online)
ISSN: 2788-7863 (print)
ISSN: 2788-7871 (online)

Contents

Introduction

IP Facts and Figures 2022 from the World Intellectual Property Organization (WIPO) provides an overview of intellectual property (IP) activity using the latest available year of complete statistics. The figures presented here are drawn from WIPO's more comprehensive *World Intellectual Property Indicators 2022*.

IP Facts and Figures serves as a quick reference guide covering five types of industrial property: patents, utility models, trademarks, industrial designs, and geographical indications (GIs). It focuses primarily on application data, the most often used measure of IP activity. Trademark application data refer to class counts, that is, the number of classes specified in applications. This affords a better comparison of international trademark filing activity across IP offices, because some jurisdictions may allow multiple classes of goods and services to be specified in a single application, whereas others require a separate application for each class. For the same reason, industrial design data refer to design counts, that is, the number of designs contained in applications.

Unless otherwise stated, all data refer to activity that occurred in calendar year 2021, and growth means annual growth, that is, the change from 2020 to 2021.

Please note: due to the continual updating of statistics, the data presented in this publication may differ from data previously published, and also from the data available on WIPO's web pages. For a greater in-depth analysis of WIPO and/or national office IP statistics, please visit the following internet pages:

IP statistics: *www.wipo.int/ipstats*

World Intellectual Property Indicators: *www.wipo.int/ipstats/en/wipi*

Contact information:
Department for Economics and Data Analytics
e-mail: *ipstats.mail@wipo.int*

Global intellectual property applications and active IP rights

Filing activity for patents, trademarks and industrial designs increased in 2021

1. Total applications worldwide, 2021

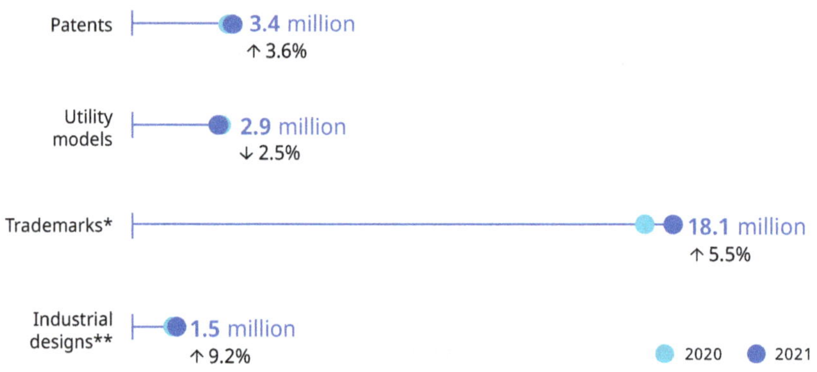

* refers to class count – the total number of goods and services classes specified in trademark applications.

** refers to design count – the total number of designs contained in industrial design applications.

Source: WIPO Statistics Database, September 2022.

In 2021, global patent filing increased by 3.6%, and trademark and industrial design filing activity also grew by 5.5% and 9.2%, respectively. In terms of volume, patent filings around the world numbered 3.4 million, trademark filing activity 18.1 million and industrial design filing activity 1.5 million. In contrast, applications for utility models – a special form of patent right – fell by 2.5% to 2.9 million applications.

Offices located in Asia accounted for more than two-thirds of IP filing activity

2. Percentage shares of IP filing activity by region, 2021

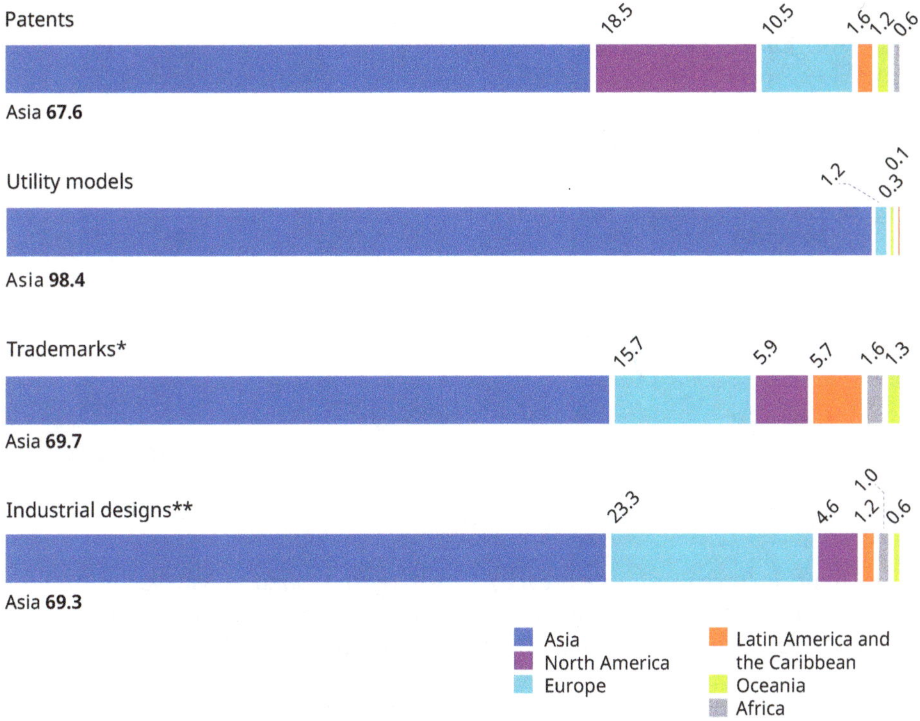

* refers to class count – the total number of goods and services classes specified in trademark applications.

** refers to design count – the total number of designs contained in industrial design applications.

North American offices do not offer utility model registration and are therefore not included in the bar for that IP right.

Source: WIPO Statistics Database, September 2022.

Offices located in Asia accounted for two-thirds or more of total filing activity for patents, trademarks and industrial designs worldwide, as well as almost the entire global utility model filing activity. Over the past decade, Asia's global share of applications filed for these four IP rights has increased considerably. For example, Asia's share of all patent applications filed worldwide increased from 54.6% in 2011 to 67.6% in 2021.

Active industrial design and trademark registrations like utility model grants worldwide saw double-digit growth in 2021

3. IP rights in force, 2021

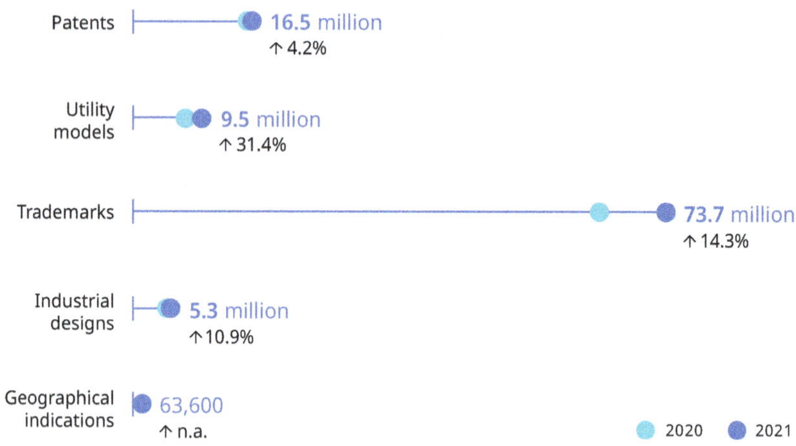

n.a. indicates not available.
Source: WIPO Statistics Database, September 2022.

Patents in force worldwide grew by 4.2% to reach around 16.5 million in 2021. The highest numbers of patents in force were recorded in China (3.6 million), the United States of America (US) (3.3 million) and Japan (2 million).

There were an estimated 73.7 million active trademark registrations worldwide in 2021 – up 14.3% on 2020, with 37.2 million in China alone, followed by 2.8 million in the US and 2.6 million in India.

The total number of industrial design registrations in force worldwide grew by 10.9% in 2021 to reach around 5.3 million. The most registrations in force were in China (2.6 million), the Republic of Korea (388,500) and the US (381,549).

Data from a total of 93 national and regional authorities show there were an estimated 63,600 protected geographical indications (GIs) in existence in 2021. However, the overall total of around 63,600 will inevitably include a degree of double counting, as GIs in force through bilateral, plurilateral or multilateral agreements could potentially be included multiple times. If GIs in force through various international agreements are excluded, then around 20,600 GIs were in force in 2021.

Patents and utility models

The top five offices accounted for 85.1% of the world total

4. Percentage shares of total patent applications by the top five offices, 2021

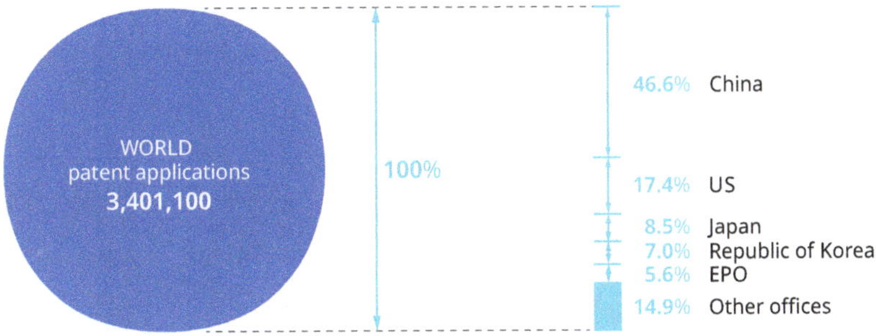

EPO is the European Patent Office.
Source: WIPO Statistics Database, September 2022.

Together, the top five offices accounted for 85.1% of the world total in 2021, 6.6 percentage points higher than their combined share a decade earlier in 2011. This is entirely due to an unprecedented growth in filings in China. China's share of the world total has almost doubled, from 24.4% in 2011 to 46.6% in 2021. By contrast, the other four top five offices experienced a decrease in their respective shares during the same period.

Seven top 10 offices received more patent applications in 2021 than in 2020

5. Patent applications for the top 10 offices, 2021

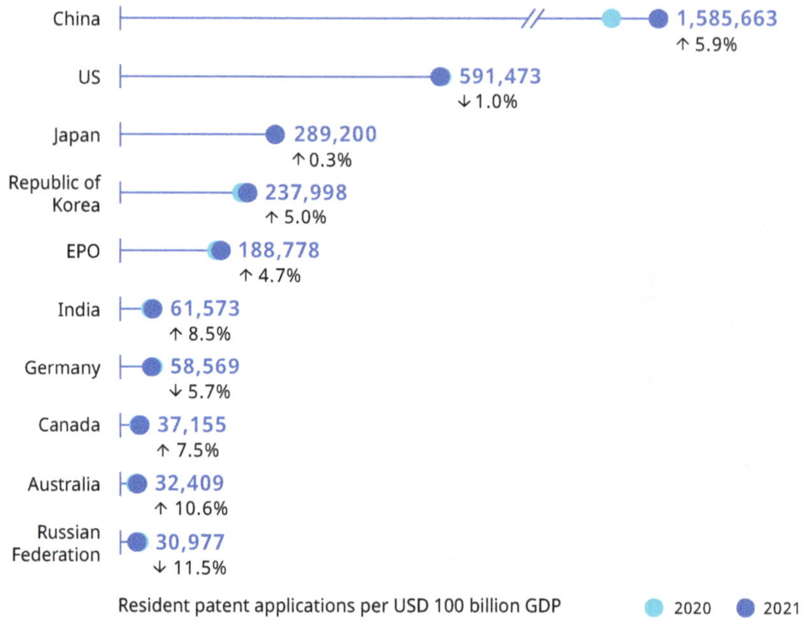

EPO is the European Patent Office.
Source: WIPO Statistics Database, September 2022.

A majority of the top 10 offices – seven of the 10 – received a greater number of patent applications in 2021 than in 2020. The largest increases were in Australia (+10.6%), India (+8.5%), Canada (+7.5%) and China (+5.9%). In Australia and Canada, an increase in non-resident filings was the principal driver of overall growth, whereas in China and India, an increase in resident filings was the main contributor.

Like the office of Viet Nam, both African regional offices, ARIPO and OAPI, saw double digit-growth in 2021

6. Patent applications for offices of selected low- and middle-income countries, 2021

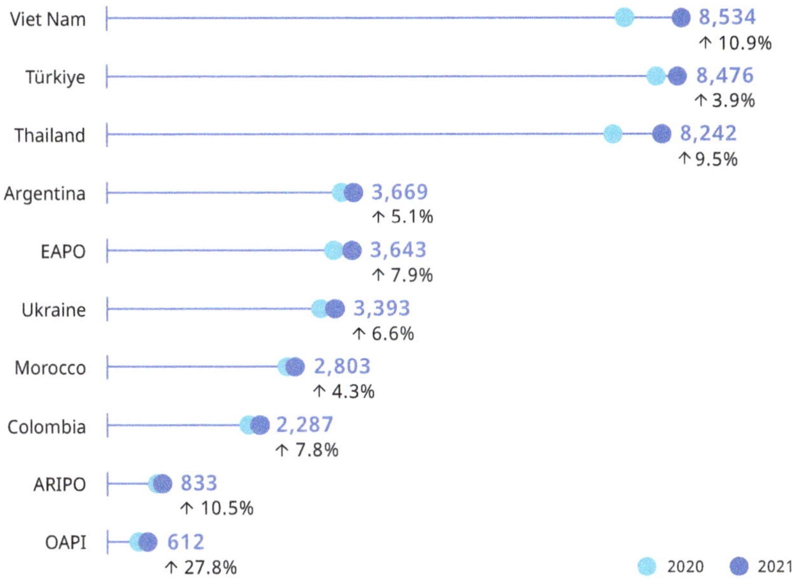

ARIPO is the African Regional Intellectual Property Organization; EAPO is the Eurasian Patent Organization; OAPI is the African Intellectual Property Organization.

Source: WIPO Statistics Database, September 2022.

Focusing on selected offices of low- and middle-income countries shows the offices of Viet Nam (8,534), Türkiye (8,476) and Thailand (8,242) to have all received over 8,000 applications in 2021. All the offices of selected low- and middle-income countries reported having received more applications in 2021 compared to 2020. Non-resident filings were the primary contributor to total growth in every one of these offices, apart from the African Intellectual Property Organization (OAPI) and Türkiye. For the number of patent applications received by every IP office (where available), see the statistical table starting on page 29.

Republic of Korea residents filed the most patents per unit of GDP in 2021

7. Resident patent applications relative to GDP for the top 10 origins, 2021

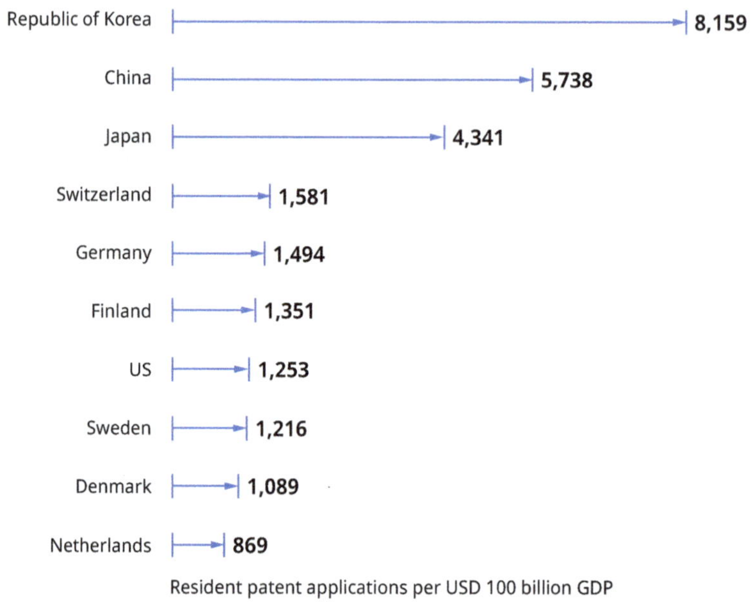

GDP data are in 2017 US purchasing power parity (PPP) dollars. The top 10 origins were included if they had a GDP greater than USD 25 billion PPP and more than 100 resident patent applications.
Sources: WIPO Statistics Database and World Bank, September 2022.

With 8,159 resident patent applications per unit of USD 100 billion GDP, the Republic of Korea continued to be the country filing the most patent applications in 2021. Its patent-to-GDP ratio is almost twice that of third-place Japan. China (5,738) scored the second highest ratio, followed by Japan (4,341), Switzerland (1,581) and Germany (1,494). These have been the five top ranking countries since 2018. Finland (1,351), the US (1,253), Sweden (1,216), Denmark (1,089) and the Netherlands (869) round out the top 10 origins. Among the top 10 origins, China has seen a considerable improvement in its resident patent applications-to-GDP ratio, which increased from 3,194 in 2011 to 5,738 in 2021.

Which countries specialize in which technologies?

8. Top three technology fields for each of the top five origins, 2018–2020

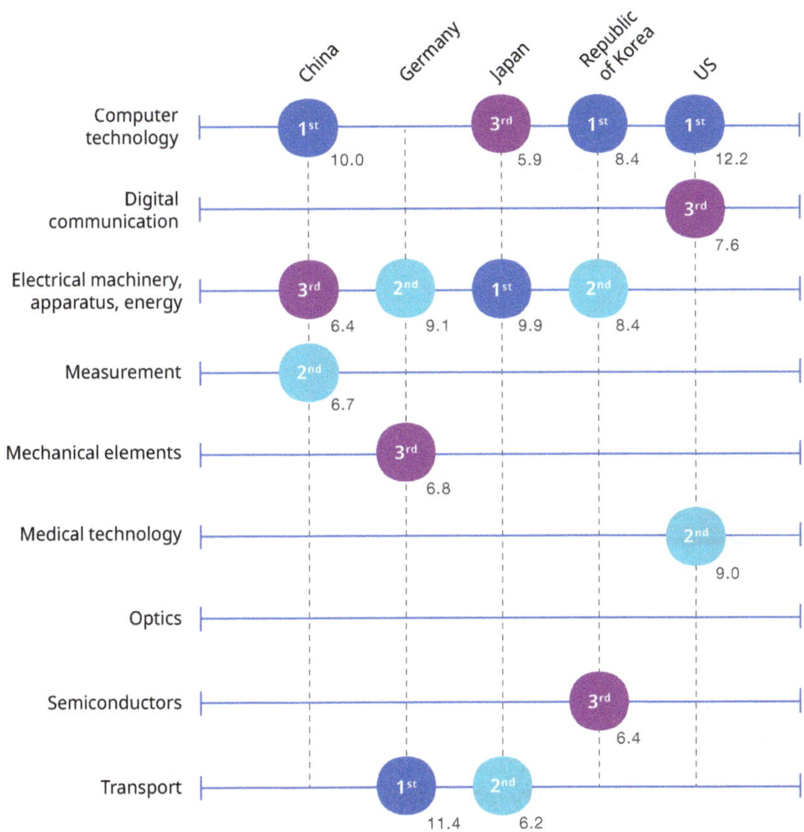

Numbers in gray show percentage share.
Sources: WIPO Statistics Database and EPO PATSTAT database, September 2022.

Among the top five origins during the period 2018 to 2020, China (10% of all published applications), the Republic of Korea (8.4%) and the US (12.2%) filed most heavily in computer technology. Japan (9.9%) filed mostly in electrical machinery and Germany (11.4%) in transport.

IP offices of Australia, Indonesia and Türkiye recorded strong utility model applications growth in 2021

9. Utility model applications for the top 10 offices, 2021

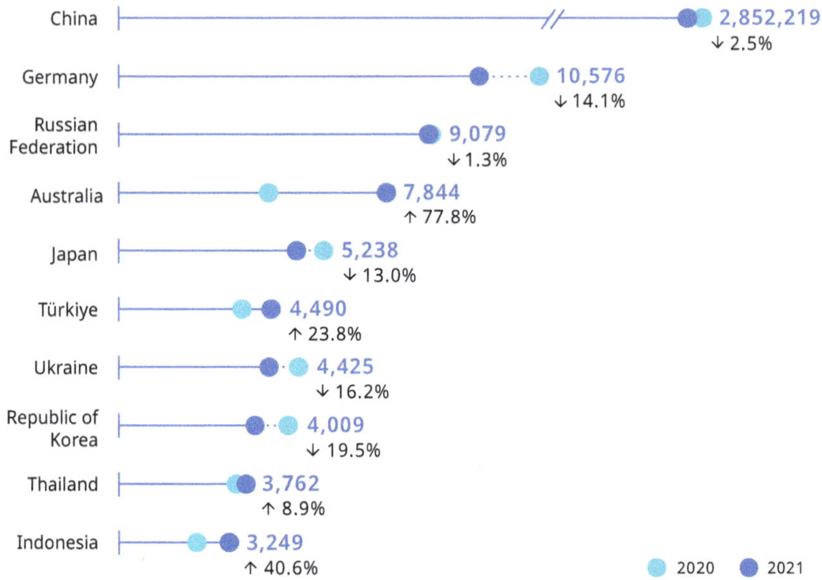

Source: WIPO Statistics Database, September 2022.

A utility model is a special form of patent right. It has less stringent requirements than a patent, but gives a shorter term of protection. Utility models are not available in every jurisdiction.

The IP office of China received almost 2.9 million applications in 2021, followed by those of Germany (10,576), the Russian Federation (9,079), Australia (7,844) and Japan (5,238).

Among top 10 offices, Australia, with growth of 77.8%, received considerably more applications in 2021 compared to a year earlier. The IP offices of Indonesia (+40.6%) and Türkiye (+23.8%) also recorded a strong growth in 2021. In contrast, six top 10 offices recorded on-year decreases in utility model filings.

Utility model filings grew strongly in middle-income countries Serbia and Uzbekistan

10. Utility model applications for offices of selected middle-income countries, 2021

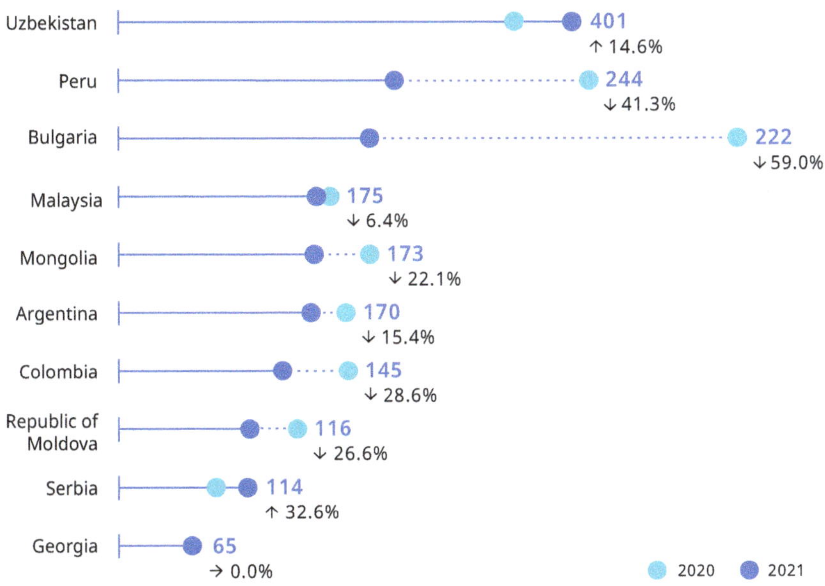

Source: WIPO Statistics Database, September 2022.

The chart above shows how many utility model applications were received by IP offices of selected middle-income countries in 2021. Applications filed in Serbia (+32.6%) and Uzbekistan (+14.6%) grew strongly. For the number of utility model applications received by all other IP offices (where available), see the statistical table starting on page 29.

Trademarks

Around 65% of trademark filing worldwide was concentrated at just five offices in 2021, up from the approximately 42% held by the top five offices in 2011

11. Percentage shares of total trademark filing activity by the top five offices, 2021

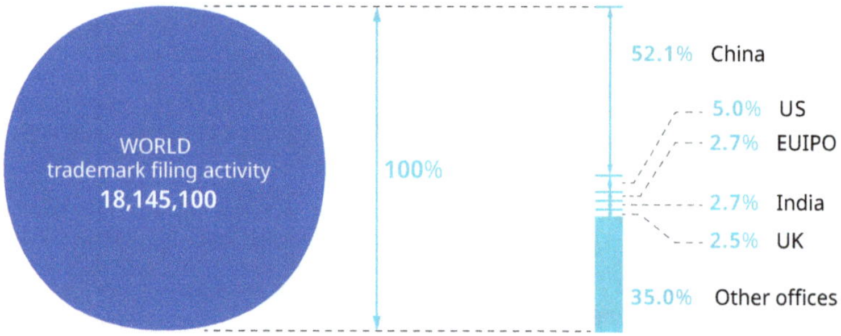

EUIPO is the European Union Intellectual Property Office.
Source: WIPO Statistics Database, September 2022.

The top five offices accounted for around 65% of global trademark filing activity in 2021 – as measured by class counts. The office of China (52.1%) was responsible for more than half of all the world's trademark filing activity, the majority of which originated from Chinese residents. The four other top five offices each accounted for 5% of the total or less.

Six top 10 offices recorded double-digit growth in trademark filing activity in 2021, with the UK (+61.8%) and Brazil (+32.3%) recording the highest

12. Application class counts for the top 10 offices, 2021

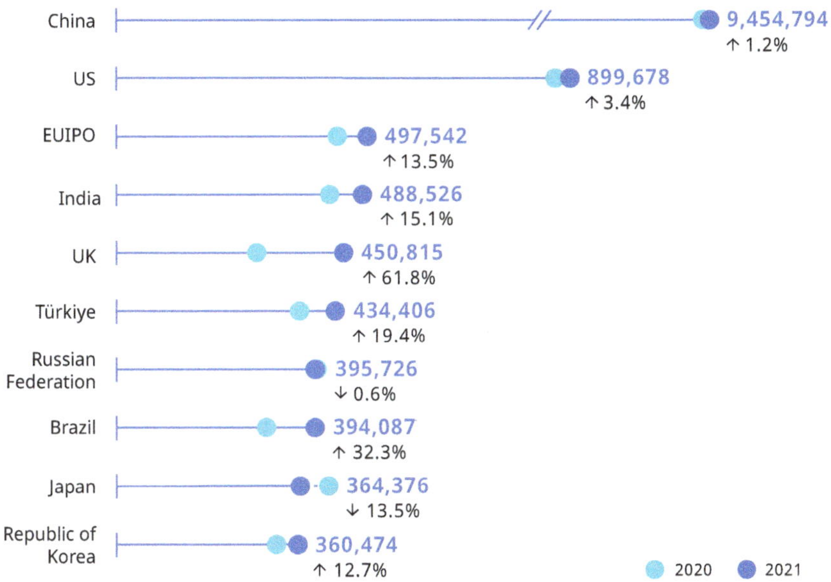

EUIPO is the European Union Intellectual Property Office.
Source: WIPO Statistics Database, September 2022.

Six of the 10 top offices had a considerably higher level of trademark filing above 10% in 2021 compared to 2020, namely, the United Kingdom (UK) (+61.8%), Brazil (+32.3%), Türkiye (+19.4%), India (+15.1%), the European Union Intellectual Property Office (EUIPO) (+13.5%) and the Republic of Korea (+12.7%).

The office of China's class count of close to 9.5 million was followed by a count of 899,678 at the office of the US. These have been the two top offices since the early 2000s; however, China's class count has risen from about twice that of the US in 2006 to almost 11 times as much in 2021. This is mainly due to the high number of trademark applications filed domestically by residents of China. These two top-ranked offices were followed by the EUIPO (497,542) and the office of India (488,526). Composition of the top 10 offices in 2021 differs slightly from 2020 in that a big increase in non-resident trademark filing at the UK office propelled it from 12th in the ranking in 2020 to fifth spot in 2021. The office of Türkiye moved up two places in the ranking, from eighth in 2020 to sixth in 2021.

Among offices of selected middle-income countries, Mexico, Indonesia, Viet Nam and Argentina saw comparatively high trademark filing in 2021

13. Application class counts for offices of selected middle-income countries, 2021

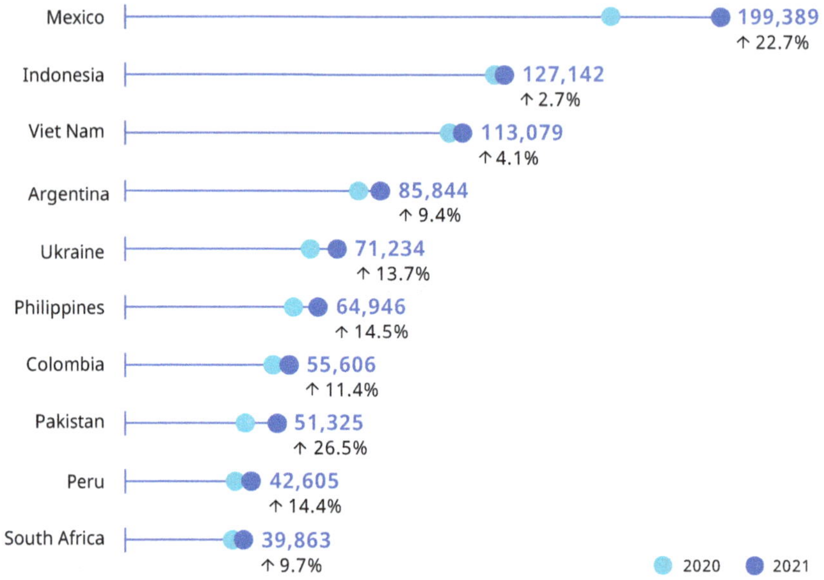

Source: WIPO Statistics Database, September 2022.

In 2021, nine top 20 IP offices were in either low- or middle-income countries. They included Mexico (199,389), Indonesia (127,142), Viet Nam (113,079) and Argentina (85,844). Other offices located in a selection of low- and middle-income countries, namely, Ukraine (71,234), the Philippines (64,946) and Colombia (55,606), saw comparatively high volumes of trademark filing – as measured in class counts. Among 10 offices selected from both the low- and middle-income country groups, annual growth exceeded 10% in six. The offices of Mexico (+22.7%) and Pakistan (+26.5%) saw particularly high growth.

The chart above shows the total number of classes specified in trademark applications received by the IP offices of selected middle-income countries in 2021. For the trademark application class counts for every IP office (where available), see the statistical table starting on page 29.

China and the Republic of Korea performed strongly in application class count per unit of GDP

14. Resident trademark application class count relative to GDP for selected origins, 2021

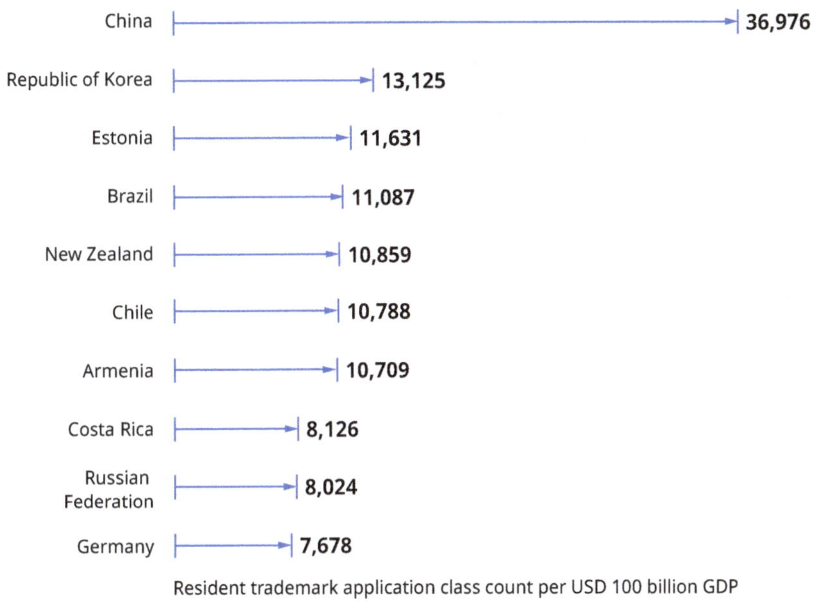

GDP data are in 2017 US purchasing power parity (PPP) dollars. The 10 selected origins were included on the basis of having a GDP greater than USD 25 billion PPP and a resident trademark application class count of at least 100.

Sources: WIPO Statistics Database and World Bank, September 2022.

Calculating application class count per unit of USD 100 billion GDP allows a comparison to be made between trademark filing activity in countries with different filing systems (single-class versus multi-class) and economies of varying sizes. On this measure, smaller countries, such as Chile, Estonia and New Zealand, rank higher than some larger ones with higher class counts in absolute terms, such as Germany.

What industries attracted the most trademark filing by applicants from the top origins?

15. Top three industry sectors for each of the top five origins, 2021

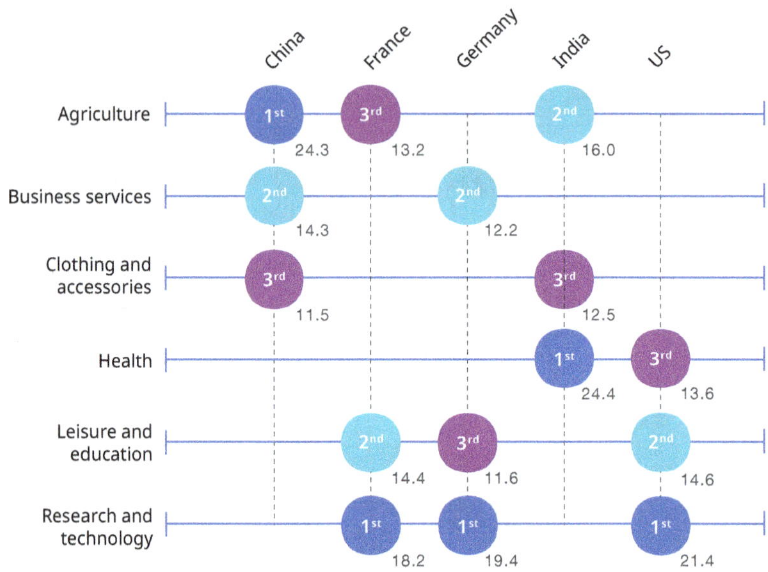

Numbers in gray show percentage share.
Source: WIPO Statistics Database, September 2022.

Using the Nice Classification, trademark applications can be attributed to 10 industry sectors. The chart above shows the top three industry sectors for the five origins with the highest trademark filing activity in 2021. Research and technology and leisure and education feature among the three sectors to attract the largest volumes of trademark applications originating from France, Germany and the US. Agriculture was a top three sector for China, France and India. Business services was the second top sector for applicants from China and Germany. Health was a top sector for applicants based in India and the US, whereas clothing and accessories was the third top sector for those based in China and India.

Industrial designs

China was responsible for more than half of all industrial design filing activity worldwide

16. Percentage shares of total industrial design filing activity by the top five offices, 2021

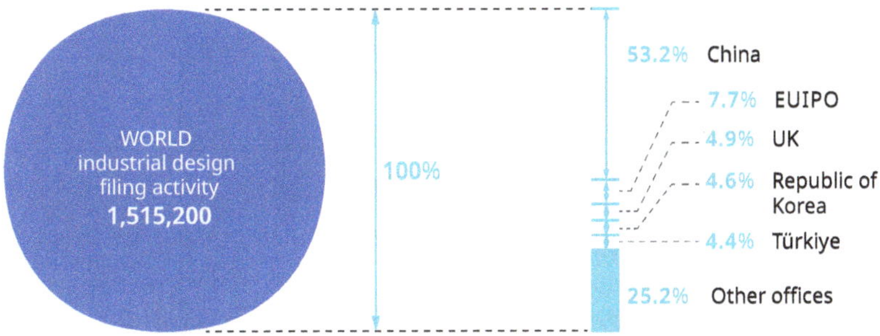

EUIPO is the European Union Intellectual Property Office.
Source: WIPO Statistics Database, September 2022.

WIPO uses the application design count to measure filing activity for industrial designs; that is to say, it counts not only the number of applications, but also the number of designs contained in applications. Design count is a better way of comparing filing activity across IP offices, because at some offices users are able to register multiple designs through a single application.

In 2021, about 1.2 million industrial design applications were filed worldwide. The number of designs contained in applications increased sharply by 9.2% to 1.5 million designs.

Almost three-quarters (74.8%) of industrial design filing activity globally – as measured by design count – occurred at the top five offices in 2021, with the office of China alone receiving 53.2% the world total. The EUIPO (7.7%) and the UK office (4.9%) received the second and third largest shares of total filing activity, respectively. The UK received 2.3 times more designs in applications than in 2020, taking it up four positions in the world ranking within a year.

Filing activity at the UK office more than doubled in 2021

17. Application design counts for the top 10 offices, 2021

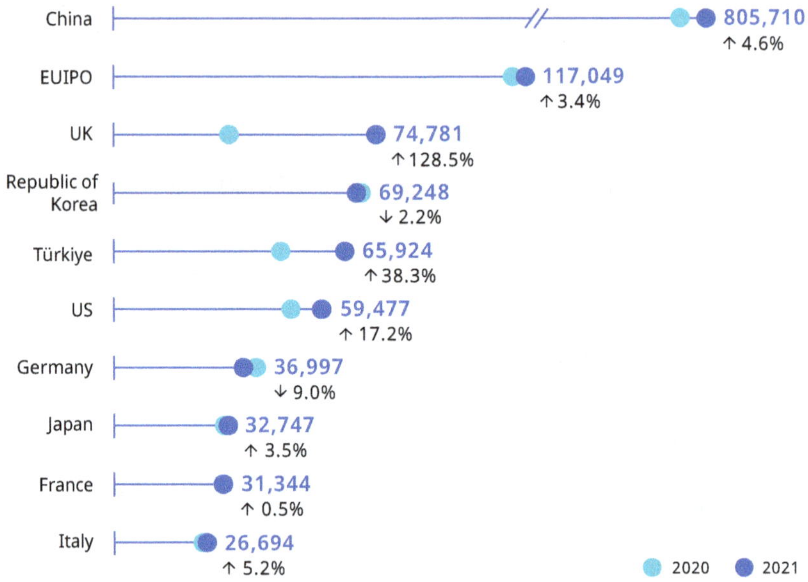

EUIPO is the European Union Intellectual Property Office.
Source: WIPO Statistics Database, September 2022.

Among the top 10 offices, the UK (+128.5%), Türkiye (+38.3%) and the US (+17.2%) recorded the strongest annual growth in the number of designs in applications received in 2021, whereas Germany (–9%) and the Republic of Korea (–2.2%) saw an on-year decline.

Among selected offices of middle-income countries, India saw a sharp rise in filings

18. Application design counts for offices of selected middle-income countries, 2021

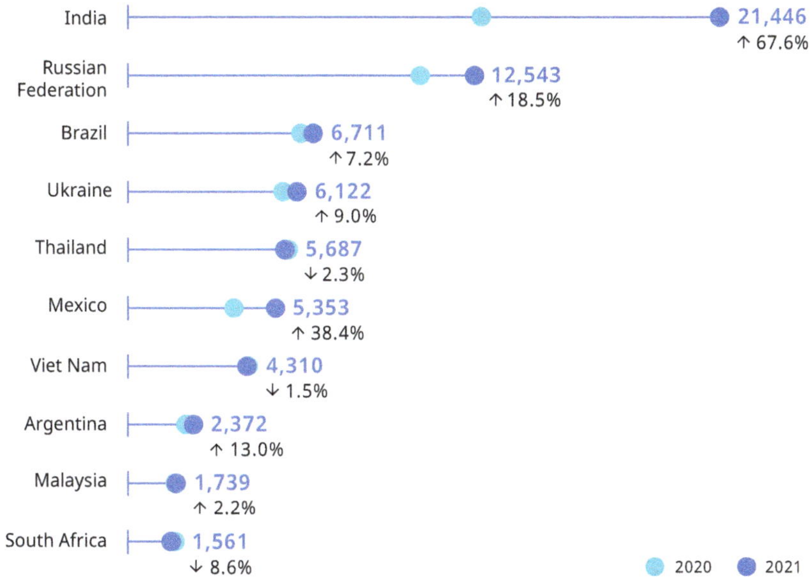

Source: WIPO Statistics Database, September 2022.

The IP offices of India (21,446), the Russian Federation (12,543) and Brazil (6,711) had considerably greater filing activity than had the offices of most other middle-income countries in 2021. Ukraine (6,122), Thailand (5,687) and Mexico (5,353) also ranked among the top 20 offices in the world in terms of design filing activity.

The chart above shows the total number of designs contained in applications filed at the IP offices of selected middle-income countries in 2021. For the application design counts for every IP office (where available), see the statistical table starting on page 29.

China leads the world in designs in applications per unit of GDP

19. Resident application design count relative to GDP for top origins, 2021

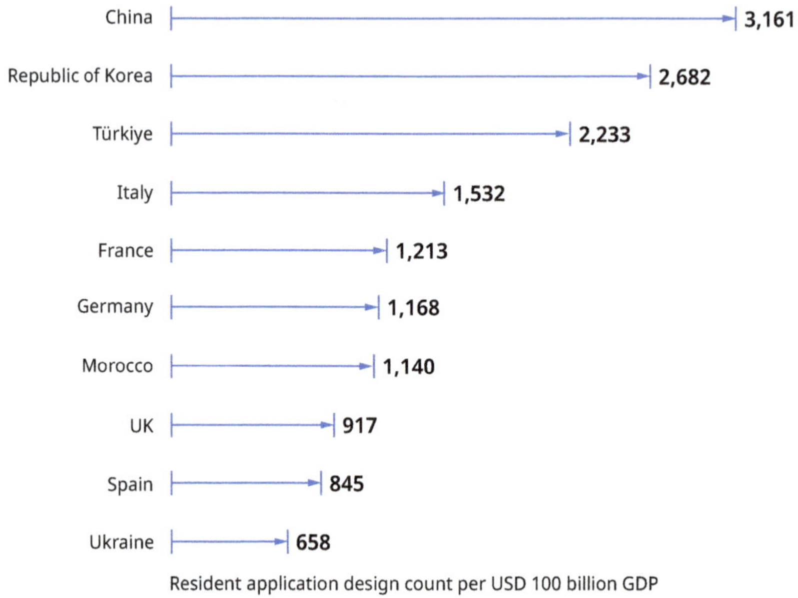

GDP data are in constant 2017 US PPP dollars. Origins were selected based on the top origins list in terms of application design count and GDP data availability.
Sources: WIPO Statistics Database and World Bank, September 2022.

Calculating design counts per unit of USD 100 billion GDP enables a comparison to be made between the industrial design filing activity of residents of countries whose filing systems are different (single-design versus multi-design) and whose economies varying in size. On this measure, China and the Republic of Korea performed strongly. Among the top 10 origins, they had the highest resident design count per unit of GDP in 2021, followed by Türkiye, Italy and France.

What industries attracted the most design filing from selected large origins?

20. Top three industry sectors for each of the selected origins, 2021

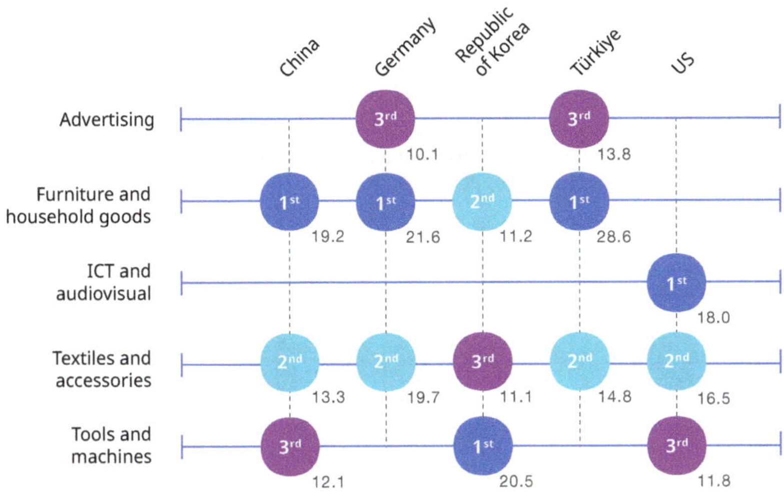

Numbers in gray show percentage share.
Source: WIPO Statistics Database, September 2022.

Grouping the 32 Locarno classes into 12 industry sectors allows the areas of strength or specialization of different countries to be analyzed. Textiles and accessories featured as one of the top three sectors for design counts for all five top origins in 2021. The furniture and household goods sector was a top three sector for four of the five top origins, the US being the exception.

Tools and machines was a top three sector for applicants from China, the Republic of Korea and the US. Advertising was one of the top three sectors for applicants located in Germany and Türkiye, while information and communications technology (ICT) and audiovisual was a top three sector for applicants based in the US.

Geographical indications

China had over 9,000 GIs in force in 2021, up 6.8% on the previous year

21. Geographical indications in force for selected national and regional authorities, 2021

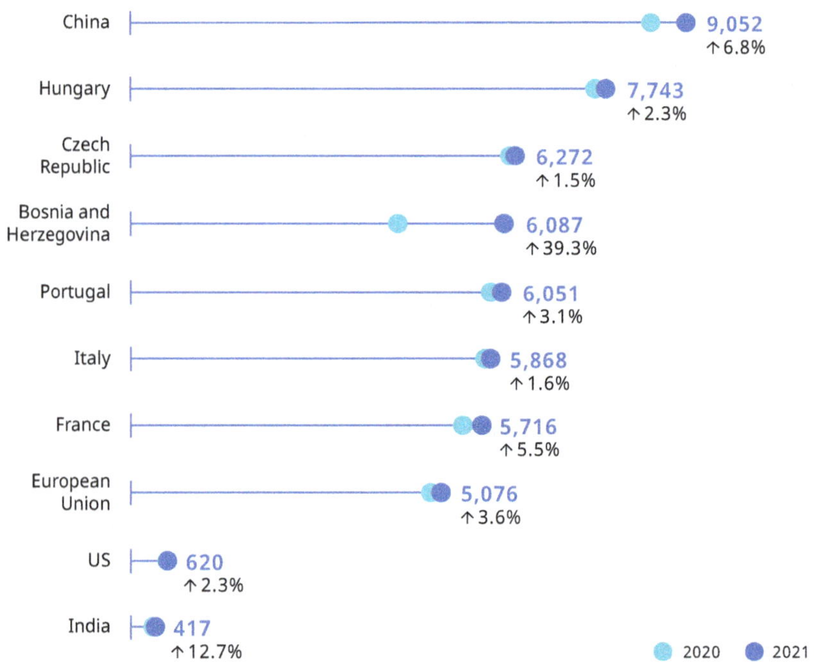

Source: WIPO Statistics Database, September 2022.

In 2021, China (9,052) had the most geographical indications (GIs) in force within its territory, followed by Hungary (7,743), the Czech Republic (6,272) and Bosnia and Herzegovina (6,087). The high rankings achieved by European Union (EU) countries is explained by the fact that the 5,076 GIs in force through the EU regional system are in force in every member state. In addition, some EU member states, such as the Czech Republic and Italy, are party to the Lisbon System; therefore GIs in force via the Lisbon System (1,052 appellations of origin and GIs, excluding domestic and refusals) are also included in the total.

National GIs among selected national and regional authorities ranged from 2.6% in Switzerland to 94.4% in China

22. Distribution of geographical indications in force by source for selected national and regional authorities, 2021

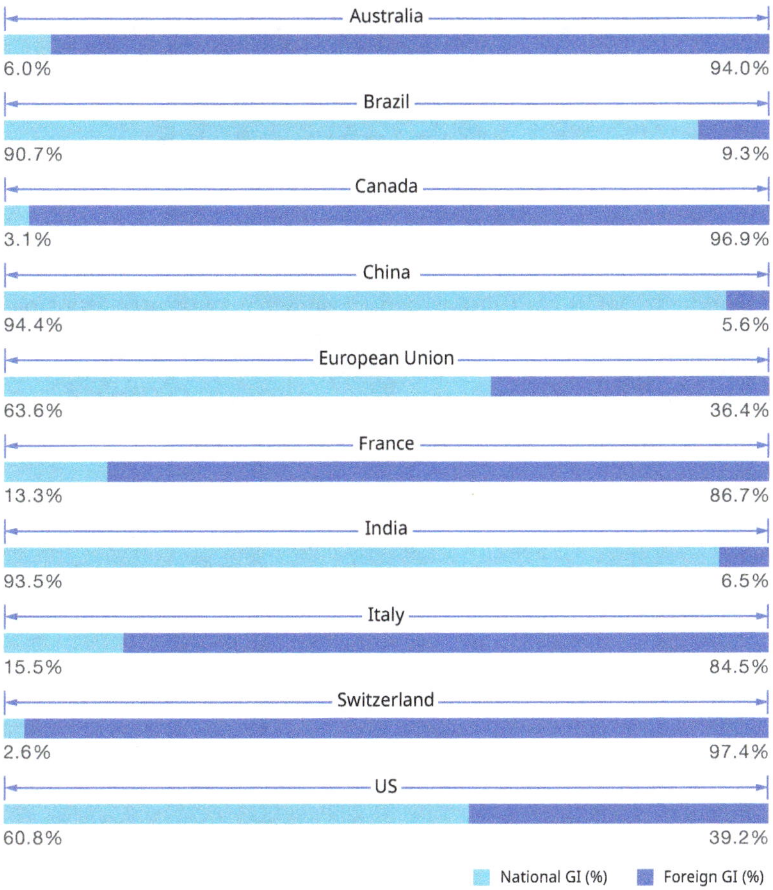

Source: WIPO Statistics Database, September 2022.

A number of authorities provided GIs data broken down according to source (i.e., national or foreign GIs). The share of national GIs ranged from as low as 2.6% in Switzerland to as high as 94.4% in China. More than 90% of GIs in force in Brazil (90.7%), China (94.4%) and India (93.5%) were national GIs, whereas nine out of 10 GIs in force in Australia (94%), Canada (96.9%) and Switzerland (97.4%) were foreign GIs.

Wines and spirits accounted for just over half of GIs in force globally

23. Geographical indications in force by product category, 2021

Source: WIPO Statistics Database, September 2022.

GIs in force relating to wines and spirits (51%) accounted for just over half of the 2021 world total, while agricultural products and foodstuffs accounted for 43.6% and handicrafts 3.9% of the total. In terms of absolute numbers, Bosnia and Herzegovina (6,070) had the highest number of GIs in force for agricultural products, Portugal (3,846) for wines and spirits and Switzerland (425) for handicrafts in 2021.

Additional information

Statistical table

Applications by office, 2021

IP office or national and regional authority [a]	Applications				
	Patent	Utility model	Trademark class count [b]	Industrial design count [c]	Geographical indications in force
African Intellectual Property Organization	612	18	15,662	774	..
African Regional Intellectual Property Organization	833	12	1,050	85	..
Albania	24	3	9,439	490	1,064
Algeria	849	..	20,372	1,161	..
Andorra	11	..	3,213	..	7
Angola	86	..	4,224	..	..
Antigua and Barbuda	8	..	2,201	1	..
Argentina	3,669	170	85,844	2,372	114
Armenia	48	61	11,878	360	3,228
Australia	32,409	7,844	174,095	8,120	2,067
Austria	..	..	..	..	5,265
Azerbaijan	135	32	14,714	660	42
Bahrain	329	..	14,132	124	..
Bangladesh	447	..	15,527	1,424	6
Barbados	73	..	987	..	..
Belarus	386	339	19,553	784	35
Belgium [d]	1,214	..	..	..	5,076
Belize	27	..	..	299	..
Benelux Office for Intellectual Property	..	..	63,753	1,195	..
Bhutan	7	..	2,211	3	..
Bosnia and Herzegovina	61	..	10,977	730	6,087
Botswana	3	6	6,003	70	1
Brazil	24,232	2,578	394,087	6,711	97
Brunei Darussalam	139	..	4,369	72	..
Bulgaria	171	222	14,987	474	5,888
Cabo Verde	2	1	271	..	2
Cambodia	..	..	12,827	..	7
Canada	37,155	..	175,907	9,491	849
Chile	3,082	113	69,115	388	1,145
China	1,585,663	2,852,219	9,454,794	805,710	9,052
China, Hong Kong SAR	21,943	552	76,700	3,858	52
China, Macao SAR	37	31	14,743	264	22
Colombia	2,287	145	55,606	952	157
Costa Rica	581	11	15,969	75	1,063

IP office or national and regional authority [a]	Applications				
	Patent	Utility model	Trademark class count [b]	Industrial design count [c]	Geographical indications in force
Côte d'Ivoire	..	..	..	..	10
Croatia	88	72	7,334	713	5,079
Cuba	107	1	5,675	15	..
Curaçao	..	..	2,793	..	..
Cyprus	3	..	3,918	20	5,076
Czech Republic	600	1,104	27,875	608	6,272
Denmark	1,276	118	9,814	320	5,076
Dominica	11	..	190	..	..
Dominican Republic	227	13	15,776	21	978
Ecuador	408	27	21,652	161	141
Egypt	2,224	8	..	..	..
El Salvador	146	..	12,778	40	29
Estonia	26	51	6,436	126	5,082
Ethiopia	..	..	..	..	11
Eurasian Patent Organization	3,643	..	..	190	..
European Patent Office	188,778	..	..	..	..
European Union	..	..	..	..	5,076
European Union Intellectual Property Office	..	..	497,542	117,049	..
Finland	1,662	259	9,323	224	5,076
France	14,759	673	314,992	31,344	5,716
Georgia	254	65	10,775	482	4,429
Germany	58,569	10,576	272,425	36,997	5,658
Greece	926	21	..	883	5,108
Guatemala	258	5	13,650	92	..
Guyana	40	..	1,215	1	..
Honduras	188	1	7,368	..	45
Hungary	446	211	12,080	907	7,743
Iceland	36	..	10,713	464	1,082
India	61,573	..	488,526	21,446	417
Indonesia	8,800	3,249	127,142	4,368	108
Iran (Islamic Republic of)	..	..	..	..	584
Ireland	117	112	8,373	114	5,076
Israel	9,609	..	26,102	1,955	930
Italy	11,078	2,019	119,578	26,694	5,868
Jamaica	76	..	6,795	100	4
Japan	289,200	5,238	364,376	32,747	..
Jordan	347	..	..	129	6
Kazakhstan	..	..	29,090	330	..
Kyrgyzstan	87	17	8,125	321	..
Lao People's Democratic Republic	..	..	..	..	8
Latvia	108	..	5,630	127	5,076
Liechtenstein [e]	..	..	9,223	692	..
Lithuania	90	..	6,620	344	5,076
Luxembourg [d]	1,553	..	..	..	5,077

IP office or national and regional authority [a]	Applications Patent	Utility model	Trademark class count [b]	Industrial design count [c]	Geographical indications in force
Madagascar	28	..	6,666	328	..
Malaysia	7,534	175	..	1,739	104
Malta	10	..	1,572	17	5,079
Mauritius	20	..	5,023	27	..
Mexico	16,161	706	199,389	5,353	1,691
Monaco	8	..	10,059	643	..
Mongolia	186	173	24,105	1,749	39
Morocco	2,803	..	35,048	4,386	..
Mozambique	46	8	6,557	81	4
Netherlands [d]	3,470	..	..	..	5,076
New Zealand	6,852	..	66,714	1,431	24
North Macedonia	42	..	10,608	622	..
Norway	1,580	..	52,580	4,404	37
Oman	..	..	15,905	562	..
Pakistan	993	..	51,325	572	1
Panama	436	4	11,735	85	121
Patent Office of the Cooperation Council for the Arab States of the Gulf	318	..	..	..	..
Peru	1,235	244	42,605	389	1,110
Philippines	4,393	1,799	64,946	1,372	..
Poland	3,488	779	42,755	2,755	5,076
Portugal	753	102	37,764	1,129	6,051
Qatar	769	..	9,587	..	..
Republic of Korea	237,998	4,009	360,474	69,248	..
Republic of Moldova	76	116	12,430	1,132	4,600
Romania	817	54	25,583	681	5,076
Russian Federation	30,977	9,079	395,726	12,543	376
Saint Vincent and the Grenadines	11	..	558	..	..
Samoa	1	..	1,620	..	..
San Marino	729	..	..	86	..
Sao Tome and Principe	..	..	2,685	..	..
Saudi Arabia	3,979	..	38,130	1,400	..
Serbia	156	114	17,621	895	1,014
Sierra Leone	..	..	3,493	4	..
Singapore	14,590	..	62,491	4,594	142
Slovakia	159	297	14,888	408	6,112
Slovenia	..	..	..	..	5,076
South Africa	10,960	..	39,863	1,561	..
Spain	1,434	3,091	82,163	12,294	5,076
Sri Lanka	539	..	9,947	139	..
Suriname	..	..	1,122	..	..
Sweden	2,196	..	19,982	419	5,076
Switzerland	1,555	..	116,581	11,808	4,342
Syrian Arab Republic	125	..	22,900	259	..
Thailand	8,242	3,762	68,103	5,687	170

IP office or national and regional authority [a]	Applications Patent	Utility model	Trademark class count [b]	Industrial design count [c]	Geographical indications in force
Trinidad and Tobago	151	1	4,505	59	1
Türkiye	8,476	4,490	434,406	65,924	981
Ukraine	3,393	4,425	71,234	6,122	3,124
United Arab Emirates	2,423	5	..	972	..
United Kingdom	18,855	..	450,815	74,781	4,157
United Republic of Tanzania	44	..	4,703	..	..
United States of America	591,473	..	899,678	59,477	620
Uruguay	..	..	11,075	..	..
Uzbekistan	665	401	18,372	273	..
Venezuela (Bolivarian Republic of)	291	..	9,522	291	8
Viet Nam	8,534	466	113,079	4,310	1,980
Yemen	42	..	6,568	80	..
Zimbabwe	51	..	4,627	..	..
World total (2021 estimate)	**3,401,100**	**2,924,490**	**18,145,100**	**1,515,200**	**63,600** [f]

a. Not all listed countries/territories/intergovernmental organizations/national and regional authorities have an IP office. Furthermore, some offices do not receive applications for some IP rights. Only those offices/authorities with at least one application filed or a GI in force are presented.

b. Application class count is the sum of classes specified in applications received directly by an IP office plus, where applicable, those specified in designations received by an office via the Madrid System.

c. Application design count is the sum of designs contained in applications received directly by an IP office plus, where applicable, those contained in designations received by an office via the Hague System.

d. This country does not have a national trademark or industrial design office. All applications for trademark and design protection are filed at the Benelux Office for Intellectual Property (BOIP) or the European Union Intellectual Property Office (EUIPO).

e. The Swiss Federal Institute of Intellectual Property acts as the receiving office for patent applications.

f. The worldwide total is not a sum of all GIs in force at the national and regional authorities presented. Such a sum would include double counting GIs in force through the European Union regional system and the WIPO-administered Lisbon System.

.. indicates either zero, not available, or not applicable.

Source: WIPO Statistics Database, September 2022.

Statistical resources

IP Statistics Data Center

The WIPO IP Statistics Data Center is a free online service for accessing WIPO statistics on patents, utility models, trademarks, industrial designs and the use of the PCT, Madrid and Hague Systems. Users can select from a wide range of indicators to view or download data. This tool is intended for IP professionals, researchers and policymakers, and can be accessed via the IP Statistics webpage: *www.wipo.int/ipstats*.

The IP Statistics Data Center is also available in Arabic, Chinese, French, Russian and Spanish.

IP Statistical Country Profiles

Visit WIPO's IP Statistical Country Profile webpages for more statistics and longer time series for patent, utility model, trademark and industrial design data. Like WIPO's IP Statistics Data Center, this service can be accessed via the IP Statistics webpage: *www.wipo.int/ipstats*.

The IP Statistical Country Profiles are also available in Arabic, Chinese, French, Russian and Spanish.

Glossary

Class count

The number of classes specified in a trademark application or registration. In the international trademark system and at certain national and regional offices an applicant can file a trademark application specifying one or more of the 45 goods and services classes of the Nice Classification. Offices use either a multi-class or single -class filing system. For example, the IP offices of Japan, the Republic of Korea and the United States of America (US), as well as many European IP offices, have multi-class filing systems. On the other hand, the IP offices of Brazil, Mexico and South Africa follow a single-class filing system, requiring a separate application for each class in which trademark protection is sought. To capture differences in application and registration numbers across offices it is useful to compare the respective application and registration class counts.

Design count

The number of designs contained in an industrial design application or registration. Under the Hague System for the International Registration of Industrial Designs, it is possible for an applicant to obtain protection for up to 100 industrial designs for products belonging to one and the same class by filing a single application. Some national or regional IP offices allow applications to contain more than one design for the same product or within the same class, while others allow only one design per application. In order to capture the differences in application and registration numbers across offices, it is useful to compare the respective application and registration design counts.

Geographical indication

A geographical indication (GI) is a sign identifying a good as originating in a specific geographical area and possessing a given quality, reputation or other characteristic essentially attributable to that geographical origin. The main function of a GI is to identify goods while informing about a connection between the quality, characteristic or reputation of a good and its territory of origin.

Industrial design

Industrial designs are applied to a wide variety of industrial products and handicrafts. They refer to the ornamental or aesthetic aspects of a useful article, including compositions of lines or colors or any three-dimensional forms that give a special appearance to a product or handicraft. The holder of a registered industrial design has exclusive rights against unauthorized copying or imitation of the design by third parties. Industrial design registrations are valid for a limited period. The term of protection is usually 15 years in most jurisdictions. However, differences in legislation do exist, notably in China (which provides for a 10-year term from the application date).

In force

Refers to IP rights that are currently valid or, in the case of trademarks, active. To remain in force, IP protection must be maintained.

Intellectual property (IP)

Refers to creations of the mind: inventions, literary and artistic works, and symbols, names, images and designs used in commerce. IP is divided into two categories: industrial property – which includes patents, utility models, trademarks, industrial designs and geographical indications of source – and copyright, which includes literary and artistic works (such as novels, poems, plays, films), musical works, artistic works (such as drawings, paintings, photographs and sculptures) and architectural designs. Rights related to copyright include those of performing artists in their performances, those of producers of sound recordings in their recordings and those of broadcasters in their radio and television programs.

Patent

A set of exclusive rights granted by law to applicants for inventions that are new, non-obvious and commercially applicable. A patent is valid for a limited period of time (generally 20 years), during which time patent holders may commercially exploit their inventions on an exclusive basis. In return, applicants are obliged to disclose their inventions to the public in a manner that enables others skilled in the art to replicate the invention. The patent system is designed to encourage innovation by providing innovators with time-limited exclusive legal rights, thus enabling them to appropriate the returns from their innovative activity.

Resident

For statistical purposes, a resident application refers to an application filed with the IP office of, or acting for, the state or jurisdiction within which the first named applicant in the application has residence. For example, an application filed at the Japan Patent Office (JPO) by a resident of Japan is considered a resident application from the perspective of the JPO. Resident applications are sometimes referred to as "domestic applications." A resident grant/registration is an IP right issued on the basis of a resident application.

Trademark

A sign used to distinguish the goods or services of one undertaking from those of another. A trademark may consist of words and combinations of words (for instance, names or slogans), logos, figures and images, letters, numbers, sounds, or, in rare instances, smells or moving images, or a combination thereof. The procedures for registering trademarks are governed by the legislation and procedures of national and regional IP offices and WIPO. Trademark rights are limited to the jurisdiction of the IP office that registers the trademark. Trademarks can be registered by filing an application at the relevant national or regional office(s), or by filing an international application through the Madrid System.

Utility model

A special form of patent right granted by a state or jurisdiction to an inventor or the inventor's assignee for a fixed period of time. The terms and conditions for granting a utility model are slightly different from those for normal patents (including a shorter term of protection and less stringent patentability requirements). The term "utility model" can also describe what are known in certain countries as "petty patents," "short-term patents" or "innovation patents."

World Intellectual Property Organization (WIPO)

A United Nations specialized agency dedicated to the promotion of innovation and creativity for the economic, social and cultural development of all countries through a balanced and effective international IP system. WIPO was established in 1967 with a mandate to promote the protection of IP throughout the world through cooperation between states and in collaboration with other international organizations.

www.ingramcontent.com/pod-product-compliance
Lightning Source LLC
Chambersburg PA
CBHW070654240926
51846CB00003BA/906
9789280535006